Contents

Finding out about AIDS

Luke was listening to the radio one morning when he heard a report about AIDS. He had heard the word before but he wasn't really sure what it meant. The report also mentioned the letters H,I and V. These seemed to be linked somehow to AIDS but Luke didn't know how or why.

▼ Luke heard a report about AIDS.

Luke and his friends were not sure ▶ exactly what AIDS meant.

Luke decided to ask a few of his friends about it. Sarah said she thought it was a disease and that whoever got it would die. Mark thought it was something that some people are born with. He didn't think it was a disease that you could catch. Josie didn't agree because she remembered hearing about ways of protecting yourself from HIV.

There is still a lot of misunderstanding about AIDS and HIV. But by reading this book you will be able to find out a great deal more about them.

The word 'AIDS' comes from the phrase **Acquired Immuno-Deficiency Syndrome**. The letters that start each word have been put together to make a new word, AIDS. Acquired Immuno-Deficiency Syndrome can be explained like this:

• **Acquired** means that it is something that you get or 'catch'.

• The **'Deficiency'** part of the word Immuno-Deficiency means that something has been damaged or is not working properly and the **'Immuno'** part tells you that it is the immune system that is damaged. (You will find out more about how your immune system works further on in the book.)

• **Syndrome** means that it is not just one disease or one illness but a group of different symptoms or illnesses.

Having AIDS means that the body can't protect itself against illnesses in the way that it should. The reason that it can't is because the body has become infected with a virus called the **Human Immuno-Deficiency Virus**. This is usually known as HIV.

What is a virus?

A virus is a tiny living thing that is so small that you can only see it through a very powerful microscope.

Viruses grow inside living cells. Your body is made up of billions of living cells. There are lots of different types of cell and they all do different things.

▼ These are blood cells seen through a microscope. False colour has been added.

▼ Here is a drawing of the inside of a cell.

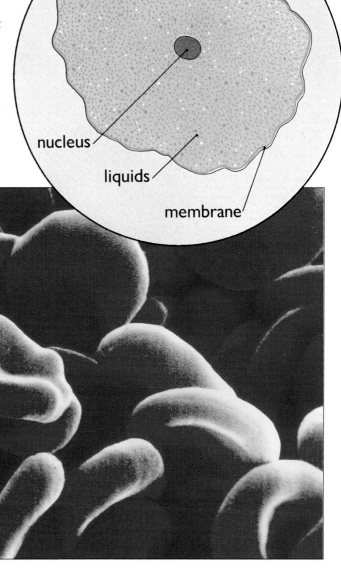

nucleus

liquids

membrane

▲ This microscope photo shows a cell making more of a flu virus.
The cell has been coloured purple and the virus coloured orange.

The outside of the cell is called the membrane. This is like the skin of the cell. Inside the cell are some liquids and there is usually a nucleus. The nucleus is very important. It is a bit like a tiny computer that controls the cell and tells the cell what its particular job is.

When a virus gets into your body it finds a cell that will let it in and it changes the program on the cell's computer. Instead of doing its proper job, the cell starts to make more of the virus. Illnesses like flu, measles and chicken pox are caused by viruses. These make you feel ill for a short time but then you get better because your body has an immune system which fights the virus.

HIV is different from other viruses because it actually attacks the cells in the immune system which would normally fight against the virus and stop it spreading.

How your immune system works

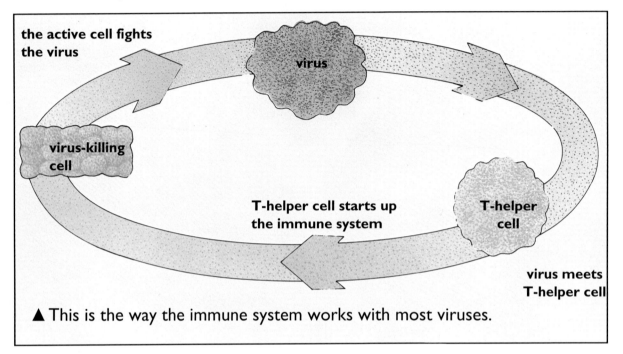

the active cell fights
the virus

virus

virus-killing
cell

T-helper cell starts up
the immune system

T-helper
cell

virus meets
T-helper cell

▲ This is the way the immune system works with most viruses.

When a virus enters your body it meets some special cells that fight viruses. These cells are in your blood. One type is called the T-helper cell. T-helper cells start up your immune system and help your body to stop the virus attacking you.

If you were to catch a flu virus, for instance, the virus would probably make you feel ill for a while. You might have a sore throat too, or a temperature. But then your body's immune system starts to act on the virus and you begin to get better.

If exactly the same virus tries to enter your body again, the special virus-fighting cells recognize it and won't let it in. This is why you can't get measles or chicken pox twice. You can get flu more than once because there are lots of different flu viruses and the virus-fighting cells only learn to recognize the particular virus that you catch.

What happens with HIV is that it attacks the T-helper cells that start up the immune system. It changes the program in those cells and tells them to make more HIV instead of doing the work of protecting the body. As the HIV spreads to more and more T-helper cells and changes them into virus cells, the number of T-helper cells in the body gets smaller. The body finds it more and more difficult to get better from illnesses because, with the number of T-helper cells getting smaller, the immune system gets less and less good at doing its job.

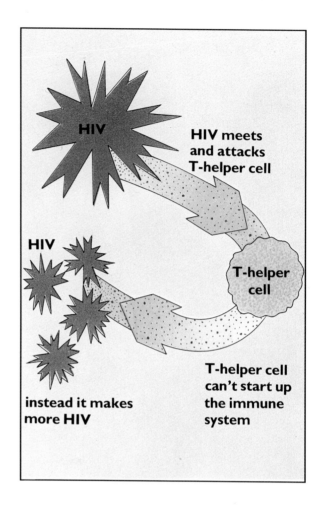

HIV

HIV meets and attacks T-helper cell

T-helper cell

HIV

instead it makes more HIV

T-helper cell can't start up the immune system

▼ This T-cell is infected with HIV and is busy making more HIV.

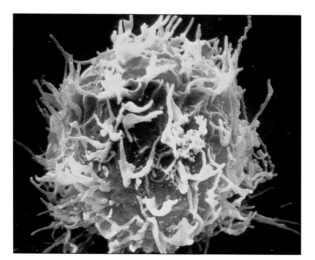

▲ Here is a T-cell without HIV.

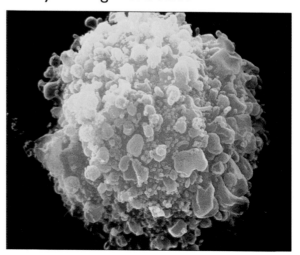

How does HIV get from one person to another?

Unlike the chicken pox virus, it is very difficult for HIV to pass from one person to another.

HIV lives in blood cells. HIV can get from one person to another if blood from someone who has HIV gets into the bloodstream of someone who hasn't got the virus. For most people, making sure that you don't get HIV from someone else's blood just means taking care in situations where there is blood around. Even if someone else's blood gets on to your skin it won't get into your bloodstream unless you too have a cut or a graze that lets it in.

So how does the virus get from one person to another?

This is Jenny's dad, Tony. Tony has HIV. Tony needed some extra blood when he had an operation in hospital. The blood that he was given had the virus in it. When doctors discovered that people were getting the virus like this they developed a way of making sure that the blood they gave to people had no virus in it. Now it is almost impossible to get HIV in this way.

◀ Tony got HIV when he was given blood with HIV in it.

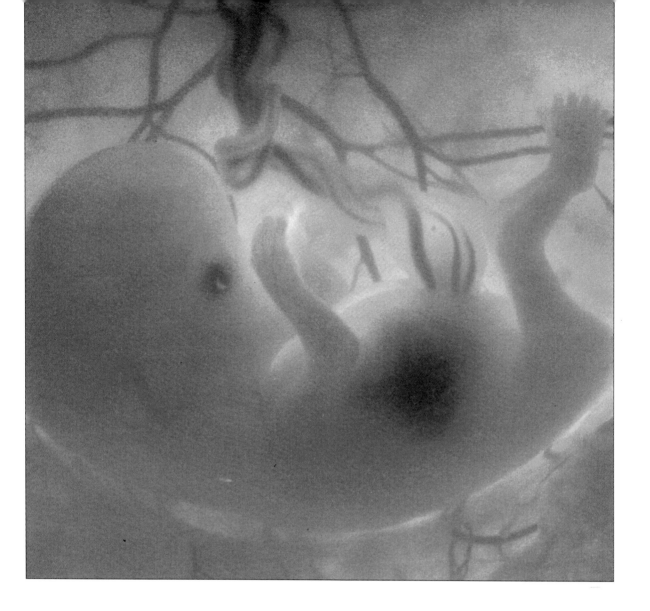

▲ Blood passes between a mother and her baby through the umbilical cord attached to the baby's stomach.

Needles that are used in injections should only be used by one person otherwise the blood from someone who has HIV might get into someone else's bloodstream.

Babies can get the virus from their mothers. While a baby is growing inside its mother it is joined to her by the umbilical cord. The mother and baby share blood which passes through this cord. If the mother has HIV, the baby can get HIV too. It is also likely that the virus can be passed on to the baby through breastmilk.

Other ways of getting HIV

HIV also lives in semen and vaginal fluids.

What is semen?

Semen is a white, sticky liquid that boys' bodies start to make as they grow up. When boys are old enough they start to get erections. An erection is when a boy's or man's penis grows bigger and becomes hard. When this happens semen can squirt out of the end of his penis. The penis then goes back to its usual shape and size.

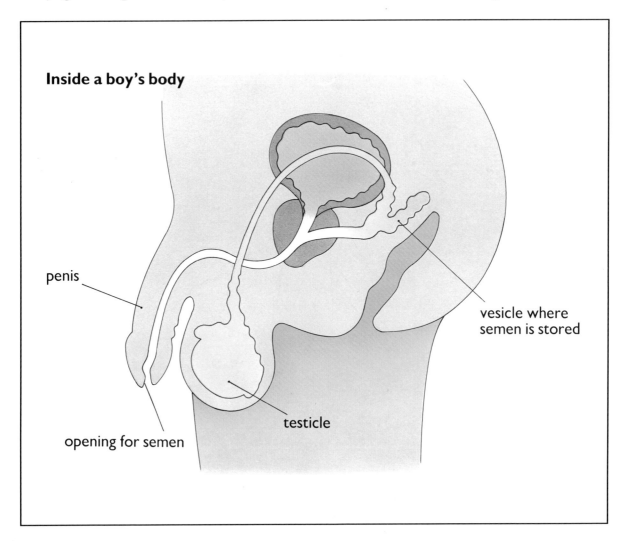

Inside a boy's body

penis

vesicle where semen is stored

opening for semen

testicle

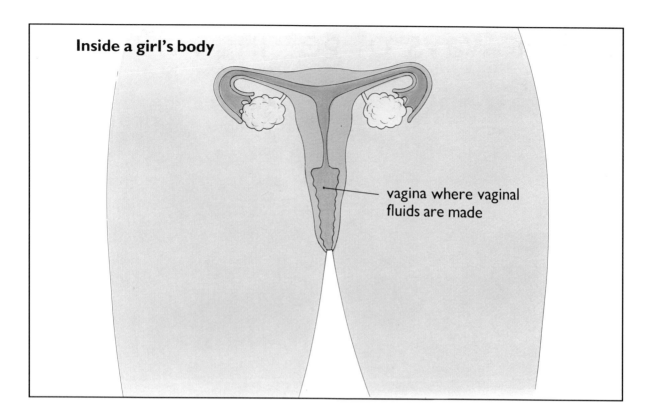

Inside a girl's body

vagina where vaginal fluids are made

What are vaginal fluids?

The vagina is part of a girl's body. It is a passage in the same area as the parts that girls use to go to the loo. As girls grow up their bodies begin to make a damp substance which keeps the vagina clean. Girls also start having periods. This means that a small amount of blood passes out through the girl's vagina every month. Semen and vaginal fluids can pass from one person to another during sexual intercourse. Lots of people call this 'making love' because it is a way of feeling very close to someone you love and showing them that you care.

When two people make love, semen can squirt out of a man's penis and into his partner's body. If the man has HIV, his partner could get the virus too. A woman with HIV can pass the virus on to a man if he has any tiny cuts on his penis and vaginal fluids get into those cuts.

Protection

Having looked at all the ways that the virus can be caught, it is important to remember that it is actually very difficult to get the virus. By following a few simple rules, most people can protect themselves from ever getting HIV.

We have already talked about the need to take care in situations where there may be blood around and we have mentioned that needles in syringes should only be used once. If you ever see syringes or needles lying around, don't pick them up. Tell an adult where they are, so that they can be removed.

People can also protect themselves from infection through semen and vaginal fluids. The best way to do this is to use something called a condom.

▼ Do not touch syringes or needles.

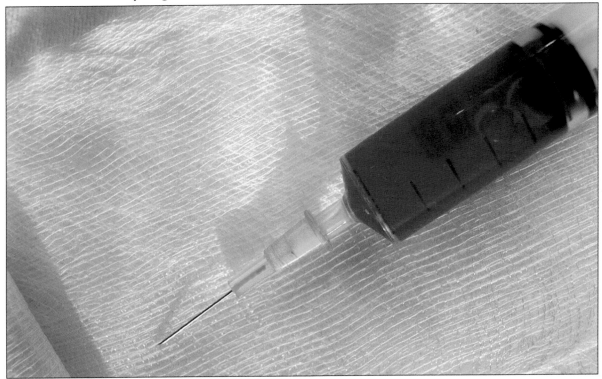

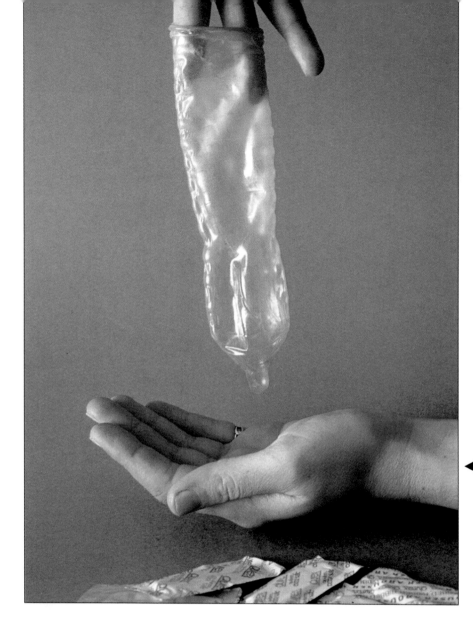

◄ This is what a condom looks like. They come in small packets like those at the bottom of the picture.

A condom looks a bit like a long, thin balloon that hasn't been blown up. When a man has an erection he can roll the condom down over his penis. Then, any semen is safely caught inside the condom. A condom also stops any infected vaginal fluids getting on to his penis.

There is now a condom for women too. Instead of being rolled down over the penis, this fits inside the woman's vagina. Although it is considerably larger than the male condom, it does the same job of stopping semen or vaginal fluids from getting into the other person's body.

Why didn't the people protect themselves?

This is John. He has had HIV since 1986. At that time John had not even heard about HIV or AIDS. HIV is a very new virus compared to other viruses like chicken pox and flu. Although most people have heard of AIDS now, this wasn't the case in 1986. You can't protect yourself from something you don't know about.

▲ John

▼ Lorraine

Lorraine has HIV too. She had heard of AIDS but she didn't know much about it or about ways of protecting herself. Talking about and learning about AIDS and HIV is the only way to stop the spread of the virus. You can't protect yourself from something until you understand it and have learnt how to protect yourself.

◄ Ben

Ben had heard about HIV and he knew about the ways of protecting himself but he thought that it was something that could never happen to him. Ben was wrong. Now he has HIV. Knowing about HIV and the ways of protecting yourself isn't enough. You actually have to do something about it.

Getting your facts straight

Alex is six years old. He has HIV. When some of the parents at Alex's school found out that he had the virus they told their children not to play with Alex in case they caught it from him.

The head teacher decided to hold a meeting for all the parents. She asked a doctor who worked with AIDS patients to talk to the parents. The doctor told them how difficult it is for the virus to pass from one person to another. He said that there was no way that their children could get the virus from playing with or touching Alex. He explained that the only possible way of getting the virus from Alex was if any of his blood got into the bloodstream of their children. This was very, very unlikely to happen. The headteacher said that Alex knew that if he ever cut himself, he was to go to one particular teacher. This teacher was trained to take special care of Alex. The parents were much happier once they understood more about the virus.

All children need friends. Children who have HIV need friends just as much as, if not more than, children without HIV.

◄ Alex felt very lonely when the other children wouldn't play with him.

▲ You cannot get the virus by being friends with someone.

▼ The virus can NOT be passed on through:

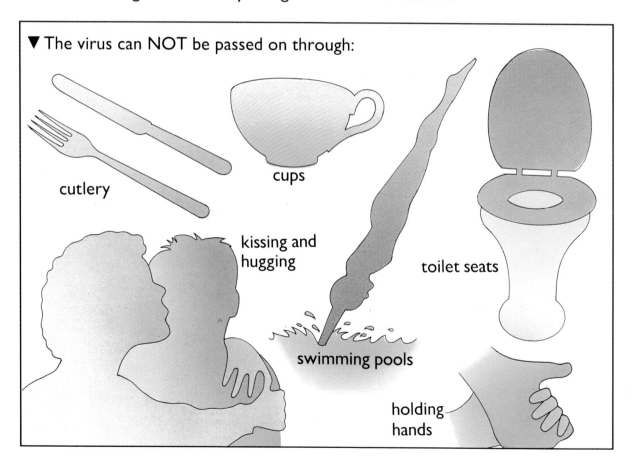

cutlery

cups

kissing and hugging

swimming pools

toilet seats

holding hands

Can you tell who has HIV?

Peter and Claire are brother and sister. One of them has HIV, the other doesn't, but you can't tell which is which just by looking. When you catch chicken pox you get spots. So both you, and everyone else, know that you have caught the chicken pox virus. But with HIV there may not be any signs or symptoms for a long time - often many years. This makes the virus very dangerous. It isn't only other people who do not know whether or not you have it, you may not know yourself. If someone has the virus but doesn't know that they have it, they could pass the virus on to someone else without meaning to.

▼ **One of these two people has HIV.**

▲ Emma was worried that she might have HIV.

There is a now a special test that people can have to see if they have the virus.

Emma had been learning about AIDS and HIV at school. She had been told that some people don't know that they have the virus and she was frightened that she might have it. She asked her mum about it and her mum explained to her that not very many children have HIV and that those that do were almost all born with the virus. Emma hadn't been born with the virus and she almost certainly didn't have it now.

Unless you were born with the virus you are unlikely to have it now. Most children do not find themselves in the sorts of situations in which HIV can be passed on. Don't waste your time worrying unnecessarily.

What happens if someone has HIV or AIDS?

It is very difficult to say exactly what will happen to someone who has HIV because it affects different people in different ways.

Having HIV is not the same thing as having AIDS. Lots of people with HIV live ordinary, healthy lives for many years. They may, however, go on to develop one or more very serious illnesses. If this happens they are said to have AIDS. Doctors have made a list of the illnesses that mean that a person has AIDS. Doctors are still not sure whether everyone who has HIV will eventually go on to develop full-blown AIDS.

Most people ▶ with HIV are fit and well. Having HIV does not mean that you have AIDS.

▲ Many of the people who have gone on to develop AIDS are very ill.

Tina has AIDS and is now very ill. Tina had HIV for about five years before she started to feel unwell. She lost her appetite and started losing weight. She recovered and was fine for a while but then she began to get high temperatures and she started to wake up at night completely soaked in sweat.

Not long after this she developed pneumonia, which is a sort of chest infection. This type of pneumonia is on the list of AIDS illnesses, so Tina's doctor had to tell her that she now has AIDS. Young people without HIV usually recover quite easily from pneumonia but because Tina's immune system has been damaged so badly, the pneumonia is making her very ill. She may even die from it eventually.

How does it feel to have HIV?

Different people will have different feelings about having HIV. This is Peter's story.

'I have had the virus for two years now. When I first found out, I was really angry. I thought it

▲ At first Peter found it very difficult to cope with having the virus.

wasn't fair. Why should I have the virus when millions of other people hadn't? Now, looking back, I can see that I wasn't really angry with the virus, I was more angry with myself for being stupid enough to get it. I knew how to protect myself but I just couldn't be bothered. One day I told myself that it was useless being angry and blaming myself. The virus wasn't going to go away, so I was just going to have to learn to live with it.

You certainly find out who your friends are. Some of them wouldn't come near me. That made me feel very lonely. But other friends were great. They were really kind and understanding. It made a big difference.

I feel much happier now. I look after my body and try to stay well and healthy by keeping fit and eating good food. Having HIV has made me see how important life is. Before I had the virus I used to take life for granted. Now, because I know that I might not live as long as I had expected to, every day is special to me. That's not to say that I'm

happy all the time. Sometimes I do feel frightened and sad but I think of how much I have got out of life in these past two years and I realize how lucky I am.'

▲ Now he tries to get as much out of life as possible.

What can be done to help?

◀ Trained counsellors help people come to terms with HIV and AIDS.

At the moment there is no cure for HIV or AIDS so most of the help is aimed at giving people information and support.

If someone finds out that they have HIV or is worried that they might have the virus they may find it helpful to talk about the way they feel. There are a number of helplines that people can ring if they would like to talk to someone over the phone.

Sharing their worries and fears with someone else can help people to feel less alone with their problems. Helplines can also give people information about HIV and AIDS.

A lot of towns now have AIDS Advice Centres. People, with or without HIV, can find out information from these centres. Many centres run self-help groups. A self-help group is a group of people who all have something in common. In this case they would probably all have HIV or AIDS. Talking to people who are going through the same things as you can feel very reassuring. Members of a self-help group give each other support and friendship because they understand each others' feelings.

There are now a number of AIDS hospitals. The people who work there are specially trained to look after AIDS patients. The people who come to these hospitals are usually very ill. Many of them will be dying. The people in the hospital try to make their time there as happy and as comfortable as possible.

▼ Concerts and galas are a good way of raising money to help people with HIV and AIDS.

The future

Scientists and doctors around the world are working hard to try to find ways of curing people with HIV and stopping the spread of the virus.

The best way to stop the spread of the virus would be a vaccine. A vaccine is an injection that stops you from getting a

▼ In the future there may be a vaccination against HIV.

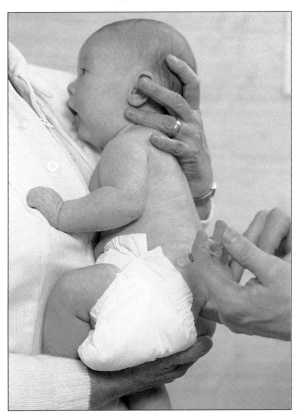

particular virus. You may have been vaccinated against illnesses such as German measles or mumps. Doctors are trying to develop a vaccine that would protect people from HIV.

A lot of research is being done into ways of helping people who already have the virus. Many different drugs have been tried. Some work better than others but none have yet managed to get rid of the virus or stopped the virus damaging the immune system.

It takes time to develop new drugs or vaccines, so, even if a doctor found the answer tomorrow, it would be a long while before that drug or vaccine would be available to everyone. In the meantime the only way of stopping the spread of HIV is by making everyone aware of the virus and the ways in which it is passed on.

Scientists are trying to find out ▶ more about HIV.

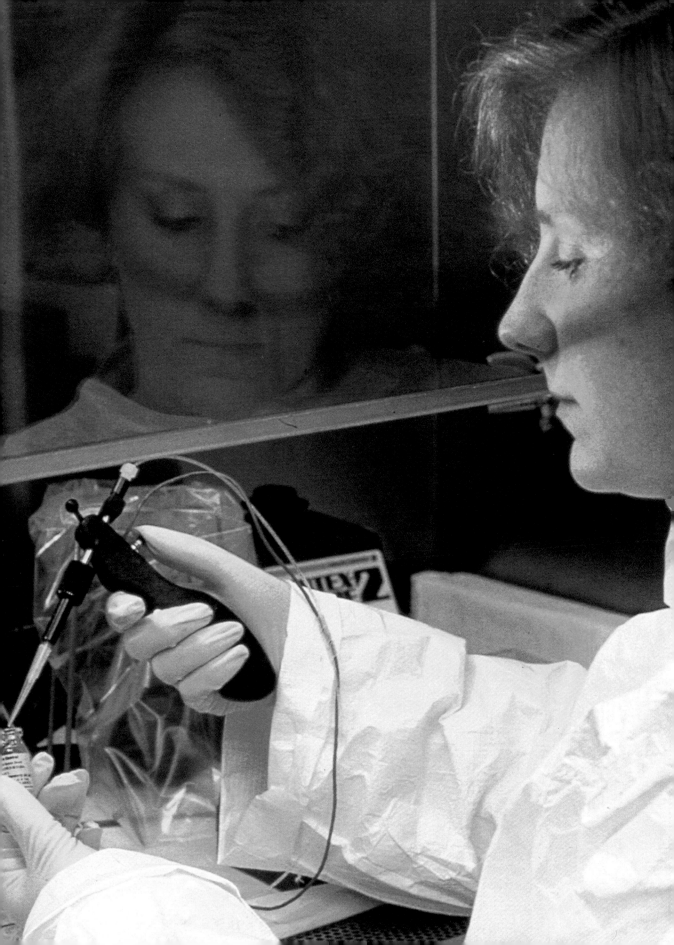

Glossary

Antibodies special substances that fight germs and viruses

Cell your body is made up of millions of these

Immune system your body's way of fighting germs and illnesses

Protection keeping yourself safe

Semen a liquid that can come out of a man's penis

Symptoms signs that you are ill

Syringe used to give injections

T-helper cell a special sort of cell that starts up your immune system

Umbilical cord a rope-like passageway that carries blood between a mother and her unborn baby

Vaccine an injection that protects you against certain illnesses

Further information

If you are worried or anxious about AIDS or HIV you can ring Childline on 0800 1111.
Calls to Childline are free.

The Terence Higgins Trust, together with Barnardo's, produces two useful leaflets called 'What can I do about AIDS?' and 'AIDS in the family'. If you would like to find out more about AIDS and HIV you can get information from

The Terence Higgins Trust
52-54 Grays Inn Road
LONDON
WC1X 8JU

You can ring their advice centre on
071 831 0330

Here are some books that you may find helpful:

AIDS by Nigel Hawkes (Franklin Watts, 1987)

Let's Talk About AIDS by Pete Saunders and Clare Farquar (Gloucester Press, 1989)

There's Always Danny by Jean Ure (Corgi Freeway, 1989)

Index